What the Water Gave Me

POEMS AFTER FRIDA KAHLO

"Pascale Petit creates forms and strategies that go beyond common knowledge of what a poem can or should do; her poetry never behaves itself or betrays itself; and contemporary British poetry is all the livelier for it. *What the Water Gave Me* is a triumph of creativity and criticism, of persona and impersonation, of personality and impersonality."
 – David Morley, *Magma*

"Petit's collection is not a verse biography, but a hard-hitting, palette-knife evocation of the effect that bus crash had on Kahlo's life and work. 'And this is how I started painting. / Time stretched out its spectrum / and screeched its brakes.'" – Ruth Padel, *Guardian*

"Dark and disturbingly beautiful in its writing, *What the Water Gave Me* is compassionate and sympathetic in representing human pain. Petit has produced a remarkable new collection of poetry, which both contributes to the artistic readings of Kahlo and presents a bleak, magnificent vision all of her own." – Zoë Brigley, *New Welsh Review*

"*What the Water Gave Me* may be an abattoir at times, but it is one permeated by sunlight... As a portrait of art itself, *What the Water Gave Me* is entirely unselfconscious and unflinching. Richard Dawkins couldn't have captured awe so succinctly. Poetry, it seems, steps in when science finds itself lost for words." – *Poetry London*

"Taking Kahlo's canvases as a spur to imagistic and abstract imagination, Petit establishes a frightening power that presses through the voice of her speaker." – *Poetry Review*

"Their apparent shared sensibility makes the ventriloquism of these poems entirely unforced, and while Kahlo's voice is subtly distinguished from Petit's own, both women have a way of taking painful, private experiences and transmuting them, through imagery, into something that has the power of folklore. They capture the unsettling spirit of Frida Kahlo and her work perfectly." – *Poetry London*

What the Water Gave Me

POEMS AFTER FRIDA KAHLO

PASCALE PETIT

SEREN

Seren is the book imprint of
Poetry Wales Press Ltd.
57 Nolton Street, Bridgend, Wales, CF31 3AE
www.serenbooks.com

First published June 2010.
Reprinted September 2010 and March 2011.

Author's Website/Blog: www.pascalepetit.co.uk
www.pascalepetit.blogspot.com

ISBN 978-1-85411-515-7

A CIP record for this title is available from the British Library.

The publisher acknowledges the financial assistance of the Welsh Books Council.

Cover Art: Frida Kahlo – 'What the Water Gave Me'
Back cover portrait of the author by Jemimah Kuhfeld.

Printed in Bembo by Bell & Bain, Glasgow

Mixed Sources
Product group from well-managed
forests and other controlled sources
www.fsc.org Cert no. TT-COC-002769
© 1996 Forest Stewardship Council

Contents

Author's note

The poems in *What the Water Gave Me* are spoken in the voice of the Mexican painter Frida Kahlo and bear the titles of her paintings. A few sequences, such as the title poem, represent one painting over several poems and are woven through the collection. Some poems keep quite close to the paintings, while others are versions or parallels. I have concentrated on the main events of Kahlo's life in chronological order: her polio as a child, the near-fatal bus accident she suffered as a teenager which left her in constant pain for the rest of her life, her tempestuous marriage to the muralist Diego Rivera whom she loved but referred to as her second accident, his infidelities, her miscarriages, the many surgical procedures she underwent, her vivacity and love of nature, her ideas about the interconnectedness of living things, and most of all, how she turned to painting as recompense for her suffering. However, this book is not a comprehensive verse biography and some aspects of her life are not included, mainly because I wished to focus on how she used art to withstand and transform pain.

— *Pascale Petit*

I lost three children and a series of other things that could have fulfilled my horrible life. My painting took the place of all this — I think work is best.

— Frida Kahlo

What the Water Gave Me (I)

I am what the water gave me,
a smoke-ring in a jar,

the braided rope
my ladder-to-the-light,

my shivering bird-heart
caught,

my mouth a bubble
of not-yet-breath,

while in my nuclei
two spirals dance,

my budding body sheathed in pearl
as I learn,

even before birth,
to doodle in the dark.

My Birth

I swivel my emerging head
so you can recognise me
by my joined-up eyebrows.

My mother's face is covered
with a sheet, so are her breasts —
they will never feed me.

Through the pink fog, I can see
with these baby painter's eyes
how bare a room can be,

dominated as ours is by that picture
of the weeping Virgin.
Even my unhappiest paintings

will be joyful. Look at how
I wear my mother's body
like a regional dress —

its collar gripping my neck.
For now, her legs are my arms,
her sex is my necklace.

Suckle

In my white baby smock
I'm pristine as a glacier.

My nurse is Mexico –
one breast is Popocatépetl,

the other, Lake Xochimilco.
I can't look at her mask

as she carries me into the studio
to paint the world tenderly

like a wise baby. I work
at the speed of light.

My ear opens its canal
to listen for the hunger-cry

perched like an insect
on swamp water, the trembling

rings of earth's throat –
when I finish those baby lips

so they can suckle.

She Plays Alone (Girl with Death Mask)

On the Day of the Dead I wear
a paper skull mask,
take my wooden tiger-head
for a walk in the mountains
where we can be alone.
Four years old, out in a storm,
lightning jigs like skeletons
and Old Baldy tells me
to stand still, holding my marigold.
I face the sky bravely, Tiger
sticks his tongue out at the thunder.
Soon it will rain – a sudden downpour –
the dead drumming the earth with their feet.

Memory (I)

Since I was six my right foot
has been bandaged in a boat.

But it's only today that the doctors
add a toy sail and smash

a tequila bottle against it
to launch me on my ocean of tears.

Roots (The Pedregal)

These rocks and gashes
are one continental plate
                sliding over another

like the very first couple.

If I'm wearing my orange dress
it's because I'm the sparks
                between them.

I fizzed out of my stone mother
                and broke her. The jolts
still rock me.

She fed me rubble,
so I bonded
with this hard ground.

Peering down a crack,
I whisper "Pedregal"
                and she echoes back.

It's enough for me to live on today,
this aftershock of a voice

that punches a hole
                through my chest

where I should have a heart.

The Bus

I have not yet caught the bus, but we are all here
ready to play our parts: the housewife with her basket,
the barefoot mother nursing her child,
the boy gazing out the window just as later
he'll stare through the smeared pane and catch
the tram's advance, his eyes wide as globes.
The gringo holds his bag of gold dust.
I am next to him, sixteen, my body still
intact when the bag explodes and something
bright as the sun fills the air with humming motes
that stick to my splattered skin. Then the labourer
with his mallet will heave the silver post out of me.
His blue overalls are clean. He is not surprised to find me
alive. Here, in Coyoacán at the stop, where the six of us
wait on a bench side by side, just as we will sit
in the wooden bus, comrades in the morning of my life.

The Bride Frightened at Seeing Life Opened

Little doll, your husband will open you
like an unripe papaya,
put a knife
to your tiny hole
and spill your stuffing on this yellow table.
No one will rescue you. Not the katydid
playing peek-a-boo
nor the owl who's flown in,
mistaking you for a mouse.

Self-Portrait with Thorn Necklace
and Hummingbird (I)

When I came to you last night in my thorn necklace
with the dead hummingbird, its wings
were flying me back to the day of the accident.
When the moment came for you to enter me
I grinned at the sugar skulls and wax doves
and tried not to think of the tram,
the handrail piercing me like a first lover,
and me bounced forward, my clothes torn off,
my body sparkling with the gold powder
spilt from a fellow passenger. In that slow silence
it's not true that I cried out. I only thought
about the toy I'd bought that day,
staggered about searching for it, before I collapsed.
They laid me on a billiard table
and saw to the wounded, thinking me dead.
And afterwards, when I came back to life,
they held a Mass to give thanks. As soon as
I could walk the first thing I did was go
and buy another toy to replace the one I'd lost.
Just as tomorrow night I'll try again
to get this sex thing right, and the night after that.

Remembrance of an Open Wound

Whenever we make love, you say
it's like fucking a crash –
I bring the bus with me into the bedroom.
There's a lull, like before the fire brigade
arrives, flames licking the soles
of our feet. Neither of us knows
when the petrol tank will explode.
You say I've decorated my house
to recreate the accident –
my skeleton wired with fireworks,
my menagerie flinging air about.
You look at me in my gold underwear –
a crone of sixteen, who lost
her virginity to a lightning bolt.
It's time to pull the handrail out.
I didn't expect love to feel like this –
you holding me down with your knee,
wrenching the steel rod from my charred body
quickly, kindly, setting me free.

Flower of Life

I flip the love plant
upside-down, release a starburst

of stamens and stigma –
insecticide yellow
to ward off scorpions

from our marriage bed.
And around the ruby mandragora
I let the rosette of leaves

bare their petticoats –
the business of what's inside
and under the fireworks.

Is that an embryo's fontanelles
in the petalled womb
or Diego's fountain-flower?

It isn't roots someone's pulled
shrieking out of the ground,

but my torn fallopian tubes.

What the Water Gave Me (II)

The water opened
into the vortex of my daughter's face.
Her skin was a rippled mirror.

She was wearing the bath around her
like a dress of glistening scales.

She was my fish-flower.

I floated on her tongue
                    like the word 'Mama'.

Henry Ford Hospital (The Flying Bed)

After the third miscarriage
what else could I do
but erect the bed-easel
and paint so furiously

my bed levitated
        out of the Henry Ford Hospital

into the region of giant hailstones
where my baby girl
floated in her altocirrus dress.

While the nopal cactus
opened its blood-red blossoms on my sheet
I painted an eagle
with its wings on fire.

I looked down at the Rouge River complex
and every factory hissed
like the steam sterilizer

everything moved like a landsnail.

I raised the mirror
and began my self-portrait.

The Bald One gave me a necklace
of desert dew.

She called me Xochitl –
            Flower of Life,
                    Pantocrator.

I flashed her a smile – my teeth
capped with rose diamonds.

Pitahayas

Here – my twentieth year is sliced
open and offered to you, ripe
as a pitahaya,
          a leafed
womb on a marble slab.

Peer into the twilight flesh
          of trauma
and the sharp black seeds
that fly into your mouth like stars.

Scoop out
the pulp with a tablespoon
and savour its queen-of-the-night
          aroma.

Fruit of the mooncereus,
having shed its only-one-time
          bloom

to hug a lump of pumice
as if it's the afterbirth.

And my daughter's foetal skeleton
standing over all this, wielding
          a scythe.

Moses, Nucleus of Creation

When a baby first opens his eyes
there is a ceremony
all the gods attend.

The sun reaches out eight hands
and the child grasps them
without burning.

Never again will light be so near.
Never again will each raindrop
hover to gaze back at him

before falling to earth.
But one day, even the sea
will part for him.

His cells are dividing, power
rises up his veins and for a while
it goes dark while he listens in.

Then his three eyes open again
and this time he sees the wind
playing along the bank.

It has all his attention, that dance
and drop, lull and leap, as if the river
is trying to stand. The baby

opens his third ear to learn water's
secrets. That's when Coatlicue
and Horus, Gandhi and Marx

crowd around the Nile,
longing for one word
from his basket of rushes.

A Few Small Nips

This one slipped out of me – my brush
knew where to aim, the hairs
caressed a zoo of pinks
and the victim's skin parted.
How heady that moment was
and how I had to keep stabbing
until paint spoke. I heard cadmium red
and crimson lake, the creature
that is all mouth was a singing cage
– my favourite brush its tongue
lapping at the misty flesh. When I finished
he was there – her killer husband,
looming over her, and I had to leave
that room my painting had led me to –
the bed with its sheet of drained arterial blue,
my own hands shaking, still hot
from jets of ruby down.
I could say how her body grew
scarlet pinfeathers and flew out
of its spattered frame, how all that remained
fluttering over her corpse was a banner
held by two bird-witnesses
with the words that he kept repeating –
"I only gave her a few small nips".

The Suicide of Dorothy Hale

Never have clouds
tried to be so solid,
wanting to break your fall
from Manhattan's Hampshire House.

The tower is trying to hide
behind the clouds,
                        which now
are feathers
from a pillowfight.

It looks exhilarating –
that descent
down the lavender sky,
the air frothy
as an epileptic's mouth.

I sit here in my wheelchair
with my baby goat
and the bottled foetus,
my paper skeleton
rigged with firecrackers
(those cardboard dildos
Diego calls my lovers).

And I'm desolate as you were
that violet morning
when the window spoke its glass vowels
        that drew you to the balcony.

The Wounded Deer

I have a woman's face
      but I'm a little stag,
because I had the balls
to come this far into the forest,
to where the trees are broken.
The nine points of my antlers
have battled
with the nine arrows in my hide.

I can hear the bone-saw
in the ocean on the horizon.
I emerged from the waters
of the Hospital for Special Surgery.
It had deep blue under-rooms.

And once, when I opened my eyes
too quickly after the graft,
I could see right through
all the glass ceilings,
up to where lightning forked
across the New York sky
      like the antlers of sky-deer,
rain arrowing the herd.

Small and dainty as I am
I escaped into this canvas,
where I look back at you
in your steel corset, painting
the last splash on my hoof.

My Dress Hangs There

The towers of Manhattan want to wear
my Mexican dress –
they feel naked with all that glass.

She was sewn with a needle of lightning.
Her lining is electric blue.
The sun and moon sleep in her pockets.

She hangs there homesick
        like a flag over the city,
without arms or legs
                        but dancing over the roofs

while my body lies on this gurney, pecked at
by the beaks of instruments
as an icy wind slices through.

The Broken Column

When I tried to dress this morning
a crack opened in my chest.

My breasts parted
like two volcanoes.

My heart glowed
like a dome of magma

inside the cage
of this steel jacket.

I passed through a shower
of white-hot nails.

What held my chin up
was an Ionic column

the surgeon had inserted
to stretch my spine.

It pressed on my crotch
as I tottered over faults

in the lava field,
the fractures grinding

as I inched forward.

What the Water Gave Me (III)

Let me tame you, my pet bathtub, and rest
inside your smooth white belly.

I'll fill you to the brim with trembling water
that's never seen light before

while you raise yourself up on your claw feet
and crawl into the cactus garden,

delivering me to my dinner guests
with a triumphant splash.

Self-Portrait with Monkeys

It's on a morning like this,
when the plaster cast has come off,
that I need to paint my monkeys
next to the strelitzia flower,

when I can feel the air
with every cell of my skin,
when all the pores
can smell the sap
in the veins of leaves,
                            sturdily ribbed
                    long as my back.

The four monkeys
are my twenty limbs,
can pick up tubes of paint with their tails
and pass me the juiciest colours.

                    My strong
flexible spine
has a tail and wings.
And every vertebra has an eye.

It's today, this very minute,
that life offers us its riches.
It doesn't matter that in the shade
the monkeys' fur is green,
that in the light
the propeller-like leaves
threaten to sprout brown hairs.

Or that my face in full sunlight
can rip open
to release the flames
            of the bird-of-paradise flower.

Roots

I've come to lie on the basalt plain
where the earth is trying to heal itself,

to peer down a rift in the mantle
when the pain gets white, keep looking

until my chest blisters – right down
where a roiling valve beats like a heart

and my own heart bubbles.
The threads of my dress

spit and snarl. I soothe them.
I calm sun flares, plasma storms.

And on the cloth of fire I draw vines.
They shoot out from my hollows –

leaves large as hands
that stroke the wound of my land.

Self-Portrait with Monkey and Parrot

I who painted this with brushes of flame
cannot tell you where I have been
this morning. But I can't silence Bonito.
He perches just below my left ear, repeating
sounds he learnt from the sun when he flew
into its core. Fulang-Chang went with him,
swinging through the canopies of fire forests,
searching for the tree that burns
at the centre of my life.
These charred leaves are the few he brought back –
they still hum many years
after my body has cooled. And you –
how long will you listen to these colours
before you hear the language of light?

Memory (II)

Isn't it enough that I've yanked out my heart?
That there's a gaping hole in my chest

my finest brushes worry?
So why does the sword of my eyes

pierce the wound? And why do I have to paint
two tiny cupids,

one each end of the shaft,
see-sawing up and down until the creaking

echoes in my deserted house
like a couple's bedsprings?

Self-Portrait with Thorn Necklace
and Hummingbird (II)

I dare you to pass my guards –
          a black cat and monkey –

into my face,
          behind which
there's a door to the room
where I caught Diego with my sister.

He is the second accident in my life.

Before a streetcar rammed me
I was going to study medicine,

had already glimpsed betrayal
through a microscope – the way microbes
          breed in a soundless frenzy.

It's time to unravel the crown of thorns
into a necklace

and lick my brush until it hovers
like a hummingbird at a flower.

Then there's a hush
in which, for a moment, I can pause.

          Listen –
it's only in the silence of this self-portrait
that the male hummingbird's nuptial song
can be heard –
          the shrillest sound in the world

like the shriek of a glancing bullet.

The Wounded Table

The table is wounded
like a wooden deer that's come to shelter in our house.

But all you do is sit in your overalls like a Judas,
a paintbrush tucked behind each ear,

waiting for me to serve chicken in chocolate sauce.
But I can't –

not with these prosthetic arms
I wave like branches.

I am my table –
her flayed feet are mine.

I race through the forest
with our last supper on my back –

Mole Negro, stuffed chayotes, National Flag Rice –
each dish pinned to my hide with an arrow.

Diego and I

Diego the glutton, guzzling monkey brains
and hummingbird hearts,

who, after dinner, releases my hair
as if opening a zoo cage

and out fly my eyes on bat wings.
And all the nocturnal creatures

that live in my mouth
burrow deep inside me, scuttling

into the slaughterhouse of my body.

Prickly Pears

With his soft painter's hands
how quickly he peels me –

like a prickly pear,
removing my thorns.

In one flash
he becomes Diego the butcher

whose third eye can see
into the abattoir of my chest

where my heart hangs
from a meat-hook.

Diego on My Mind

Today I chose the ceremonial *huipil*
with a lace cobweb framing my face.

I have made a fine bed for you
with the white frills of my Tehuana headdress.

And on the counterpane of my brow
      just where the pillows would rest
I have painted your portrait.

All day you keep me company
as I work each gauze bud
into a stiff flower.

You whisper encouragements from the mirror,
nestling deeper into my forehead.

But remember, when you take
     María Félix
          Paulette Goddard
               or my sister

to your dirty yellow hotel room,
they lie on my eyes.

My nose smells them.
My mouth stays closed. Every love-cry

is a silk tendril
      quivering in my silent house.

Self-Portrait with Cropped Hair

There was a grinding of black blades
in that sixth room of hell
I fell into after you left.
I sharpened the scissors until
my bedroom became the House of Knives.

Then I sat on the crazy-yellow chair
and watched my snake-locks rise
from the floor, dance like musical staves
and sing that old folksong you used to whistle –

Look, if I love you, it is for your hair,
now you are bald I love you no more.

Light (Fruit of Life)

The sun sits on my bedside table
like an orange spider,
entangling my still life in his rays.
He has Diego's features.

My own portrait is buried
in the flesh of a melon
but I haven't the strength
to excavate it.

And the mamey fruit,
        the pitahayas –
what do they contain?

My bride doll and sugar skeleton
sit on a banana
contemplating red rinds
sliced open –
                white universes
packed with black stars,

so amazed
at this morning's bounty
that for once
they are not afraid of each other,
are holding hands.

I have placed her doll bed
next to his candy coffin.
Tonight they'll sleep together
like an old married couple.

Two Nudes in the Forest (Earth Herself)

After I cleared the earth from her mouth
I pushed my hand in. Her lips
were a bracelet around my wrist
as I drew birdsong from her throat.
I swam along the vertigo of vines
that were her veins, plunged myself
into her hide. Her waist was just a scrawl
of rough strokes, the paint lithe with streaks
through which the forest glowed.
We lay there with our legs
twined in a plaited tail, our raft
swept up love's steep river,
while mangroves and spider monkeys
slid over us in a tapestry of light.

The Two Fridas

I snap the stem
of another vial of Demerol,
inject it into my back

then choose my white lace dress –
the one with a starched collar
    and little rosebuds splashed on the hem –

to wear over the plaster corset
painted with a foetus,
        a hammer and sickle.

              ★

The thousand shattered pieces of the street
re-assemble on these metal sheets
where I paint my *retablos*.

By late afternoon, I can make
the rain fall upwards, back
to the sky of my girlhood.

The room bends like a bus hit by a tram.
It wobbles. Straightens.
The post piercing my pelvis
pulls itself out.

              ★

The second Frida sits next to me
like another passenger, her knee touches mine.
We chat about our lives.
She describes the picture I cannot paint –
the day
        night fell in my life.

She says it's a double self-portrait:
a bride with a strong girl
from the matriarchal Zapotec tribe.

Her palette is my heart sliced in half.

I place my hand in the hole
behind my breasts,
feel the half I've had to make do with.

Strange how it keeps beating,
turning blood to paint.

What the Water Gave Me (IV)

The bath I lie in like a sarcophagus,
the water that's about to become kerosene,
the surface I have to keep absolutely still
so my body can slip through it
like a reflection passing out of a mirror,
the skin that's been softening all night,
my nerves coiled tight as a moth's proboscis,
the worms parading on tightropes,
the tiny ballerina of my soul
tiptoeing down a spider's web tied from my neck,
the ulcers and craters, the giant
one-legged quetzal pierced by a tree,
my toes and their doubles, their blood-red nails,
the ex-votos to give thanks for surviving
twenty-two fractures, the miniature parents
on their atoll far off as my thigh,
the Empire State Building spewing gangrene
over my shin, that no perfume can mask
so no one will visit,
the life lived dying,
the head cracked open,
my half drowned thoughts bobbing around my legs,
the face floating near my knee like a blouse,
the herbal water that enters my pores hour by hour,
that just before dawn sings with the voice of a snowflake
so that my ghost starts to lift from my flesh,
but the visions keep calving
like bergs of trolley-bus glass –
that moment I stopped being a child
and grew old in seconds,
how I can see through the white enamel arch
into a transparent planet
while, in slow-motion waves,
a steel handrail breaks off and hurtles towards me.

The Love Embrace of the Universe, the Earth (Mexico), Diego, Myself and Señor Xólotl

When you came back to me –

I painted a green day-hand and a brown night-hand
holding up Mexico, her canyons and deserts,
        her candelabra cacti.

And we were there, embraced by our land.
You were my naked baby
who is reborn every minute with your third eye open.

Even our dog Señor Xólotl was curled
on the wrist of evening,
ready to bear our souls to the underworld if he had to.

Together, we stared out beyond the picture, saw
in the dark window a small woman in a wheelchair
cast out in a workshop far beyond the moon,

desperately mixing the colours of love
        until they vibrated –
watermelon greens, chilli reds, pumpkin orange.

She hurriedly drew the shattered arms
of the universe –
                holding us all up

as if we were a mountain dripping roots and stones.

Memory (III)

My dresses are lowered from the clouds.
The sky's wardrobe is open, the mirror of twilight

shivers with stars where seamstresses
quickly sew, snipping each thread

with haemostatic scissors. And just
as night falls, my school uniform

and Tehuana gown each offer me an arm.
As we walk, those seraphim clothes

speak in silk and velvet voices –
rustles from the cloth of memory.

Tree of Hope, Stand Fast

Those bastard surgeons
messed with my spine
then wheeled me out onto an earthquake floor
and left me there.

The sun prised open my scars.

From my blood I stitched a crimson dress
and sat next to myself on guard.

I placed my painting-fingers in the ditch
and touched the root-nerve of the earth

down where mountains are born
from boiling rock
                until a vent

gushed open
and the molten stream
set into this hard corset.

All week I sat there at my vigil,
praying that it would twine
around my ribs
              like a tree of hope,
holding my back firm.

The Little Deer

Little deer, I've stuffed all the world's diseases inside you.
Your veins are thorns

and the good cells are lost in the deep dark woods
of your organs.

As for your spine, those cirrus-thin vertebrae
evaporate when the sun comes out.

Little deer too delicate for daylight,
your coat of hailstones is an icepack on my fever.

Are you thirsty?
Rest your muzzle against the wardrobe mirror

and drink my reflection –
the room pools and rivers about us

but no one comes
to stop my bed from sliding down your throat.

Self-Portrait with Thorn Necklace
and Hummingbird (III)

Into my studio my hummingbird comes.
Through the whirr of his body the life force surges.

My father's creative breath blows
through his feathers

to make my art live
long after my death.

My hummingbird is an Aztec war god
and I give myself to him daily.

His bill is the sword
that once pierced my vagina.

His tongue sucks the juice of each hour
        (he drinks light)
        (he never knows thirst).

His shield is my palette
and I work only when he sings.

He is my wizard, my precious son.

Every morning he springs fully formed
from my thighs
to battle with my sickness.

When my painting is done
he hangs himself from my neck
on a garland of thorns.

I am my hummingbird.

Portrait of Mariana Morilla Safa

You come fresh from the battlefields of your childhood,
trailing the city behind you

like a bridal train
so Fridita can smell the avenues tangled in your wake –

my kid-soldier of the sun
in petal pink,
eager to play Flower Wars with me.

In my wardrobe
you'll find all the costumes
for the seven underworlds

a Jaguar Warrior must brave
but don't let that fierce mask bite your face.

Be my keeper of the night terrors,
guardian of the bowl of fatigue.

Tonight, I'll be the butterfly Xochiquetzal
and perch on that silk bow in your hair
as you skip back home through Coyoacán Square.

The Dream

It's so easy to slip through the hole
a needle makes,
my bed crashing through the ceiling
to ascend like a kite in a gale,
the god of lightning on my canopy
with his cardboard skyrockets,
his pyrotechnics,
the vine of life electrocuting me as I soar,
but still I don't wake,
even when the clouds turn into nurses
shaking me from surgery,
I, the atrocity,
more naked than a human should be,
thinner than a thunderclap,
the altitude embalming my face with ice,
the sudden release
as I'm pelted by spears of rain –
each drop long as a syringe
in which my bed is trapped.

The Plane Crash

Their bodies have hit the tarmac
but their shrieks still float
in the subzero air. I have to wade
through the jet fuel, my canvas
bursting like an eardrum. Fumes
warp the ether like a looking-glass
I grasp each morning and shake.
And there's a face I can't clean, however hard
I scrape with the palette knife
or part the scorched hair. Doctor Eloesser
beckons me, the flame-roar is my signal.
He wants me to use my art to save lives.
My bedroom is always recovering
from the blast but I paint on; a sling
hooked around my chin holds my neck
up to the bed-easel at just the right angle.
All my life I have been stumbling
down the incandescent aisles
of a plummeting aircraft, sketching
my fellow passengers braced for impact.
And no matter how many bubbles I draw
trailing from mouths, no one
rises from the wreckage to greet me.

Fruits of the Earth

Little peg-leg stuck in a bowl of fruit
with towering mushrooms dripping honey.
I'll nibble a piece of their flesh
and dance on my bandaged stump.
Then the green cobs will turn into men
sweet as the first corn people.
I'll dance with each one
even if I stink like a rotting sapodilla –
that's how raw the night's become,
with its browning cherimoya
and those skinned prickly pear hearts.
I press myself into their pulp – the girl
who once glimpsed a woman running
down the street with her intestines in her hands,
holding them up like the fruits of the earth.

Self-Portrait with Monkey

The bristles on my brushes work
like furtive birds. Hours pass.
When the painting starts to rustle,
Fulang-Chang grips my neck,
too frightened even to yelp. As if
the leaves are hiding a forest floor
where I have buried a troop of monkeys
alive. As if the only sound in this
whole house is the breathing of animals
through thin straws; even tonight,
when it's too late, and I am long dead.
And you, brave viewer, meet my gaze.

What the Water Gave Me (V)

The water enters my pores gently.
When it sings all my body listens,
the little hairs dawdle
        in calm eddies.

It is like painting then, that lost hour
when the colours play together
before becoming a mouth,
the rough face
           not yet human.

One eye drowning in its rockpool
finds a tunnel of rippled light
and opens
to gaze at its maker.
              And I,
all alone with my painted bath,
my one-thread brush
grafting skin,

my sea-changed skeleton
        a surprise reef
where fingers of live coral
knit the shattered spine.
My out-of-the-frame head
        not throbbing now.

The water a poured mirror, its song
rising up the chromatic scale
to create land on the surface.

The currents shiver like shaken glass
splashing my legs with shoals of pigment –

the blue sting, the red ache,
how art works on the pain spectrum.

Sun and Life

In the maize field I found the sun,
his warning eye open.
From this cauldron
one tear hangs
holding the world's oceans

while all around, the corn sways
huge as solar systems
and an embryo in its husk
grows a mountain range
on its spine.

I am down under the stems,
my face on fire,
but I keep on looking
into the hub of creation, stars
spinning from my brush.

Still Life

The sun and the moon
have shrunk

to the size of an orange
and a pomegranate.

They hover above
my bedside table

daring me to taste them.

Without Hope

A funnel has been shoved into my mouth
through which I am force-fed the sky.
I have eaten slaughtered angels, thunderheads.
And now they are mashing up the stars
into baby gruel.
"You can eat anything," the doctors say,

so I vomit offal, catfish.
I even bring up my own skull.
And the sky eats it. Clouds
grow teeth and patches of my skin.
I have a double, fat as the dawn.
Her belly presses on my face.

And underneath this sheet embroidered
with atoms, I am naked
as the day of the accident,
waiting for the sun's rays
to cut me open.

       The moon
watches all this, hungry as an ulcer.

The Blue House

My pelvis is a palette
                on which night
is mixing day's colours.

Yellow is iodine,
white a sugar skull
with my name on its forehead.
Nothing is black, really *nothing*.

There are no shadows in this house,
only monkeys and parrots,
only Granizo my pet fawn –
                he is my right foot.

But over there, in the corner,
is my red boot with bells,
to cover my prosthesis.

And time?
                What colour is time?
Time is a green bus where I lie at an angle,
pierced by a purple pole.

Time is my orange womb, skewered
on a cobalt trolley.

And this is how I started painting.
Time stretched out its spectrum
and screeched its brakes.

Living Nature

I have been hung naked, head down.
I have had my right leg amputated.
My back smells like a dead dog.

It is six o'clock in the morning
and the turkeys are singing.
Can you hear them
        Old Buck Tooth?
                Fucked One?
                        Belle of the Ball?

I am painting myself,
                Hairless Bitch,
with the blood of prickly pears,
the spilled reds of pomegranates,

in my old leather diary
that once belonged to John Keats –

on pages sweet as coconut milk,
                    fresh from paradise.

Self-Portrait with Dog and Sun

This is the last self-portrait,
which is why Señor Xólotl, my beloved dog,
is with me.

We are both wearing blue necklaces.
        His are the eyeballs
        underworld dogs wear.
Mine are of such transparent stones,
it's like wearing a string of sunny days.

My dress is sun-red
because I want to die at noon
        when the colours are hottest.

At that moment, Señor Xólotl
will fetch my right foot
which he has buried in the garden.
And I will be whole again.

Threaded through my hair,
                like sunrays,
are silk ribbons –
their greens and reds barking

        as only paint can,
happy as a dog with its mistress.

What the Water Gave Me (VI)

This is how it is at the end –
me lying in my bath
                              while the waters break,
my skin glistening with amnion,
                                        streaks of starlight.

And the waters keep on breaking
as I reverse out of my body.

My life dances on the silver surface
where cacti flower.

The ceiling opens
                      and I float up on fire.

Rain pierces me like thorns. I have a steam veil.

I sit bolt upright as the sun's rays embrace me.

Water, you are a lace wedding-gown
I slip over my head, giving birth to my death.

I wear you tightly as I burn –
                              don't make me come back.

Acknowledgements

Many thanks to the editors of the following, in which some of these poems first appeared: *Agenda*, *American Poetry Review*, *Antología Letras en el Golfo* (Mexico), *The Canary*, *Cimarron Review*, *Contemporary Literary Horizon* (Romania), *Cutthroat*, *Fragments from the Dark*, *Free Verse*, *The Gift*, *Helicon Poetry Journal* (Israel), *International Literary Quarterly*, *Magma*, *Mslexia*, *New Welsh Review*, *Not a Muse* (Hong Kong), *Panorama* (Bulgaria), *Pendulum: The Poetry of Dreams*, *Poetry London*, *Poetry Monthly* (China), *The Poetry Paper*, *Poetry Review*, *Poetry Salzburg Review*, *Poetry Wales*, *Pratik* (Nepal), *The Pterodactyl's Wing*, *Quadrant* (Australia), *Roundyhouse*, *Savremennik* (Bulgaria), *Shi Xuan Kan* (China), *Tabla* and *The Wolf*. I am enormously grateful to Arts Council England for an award, to the Society of Authors for a grant and to the Royal Literary Fund for a Fellowship at Middlesex University 2007–09, all of which enabled me to finish this book.

Fourteen of these poems previously appeared in a pamphlet *The Wounded Deer – Fourteen poems after Frida Kahlo*, a first stage winner in the Poetry Business Book and Pamphlet Competition 2004, which was published by Smith Doorstop in 2005 and launched at Tate Modern in the 2005 *Frida Kahlo* exhibition. I'd like to thank Jennifer Clement for my first visit to the Casa Azul in Coyoacán and for telling me how Kahlo used to leave dinner parties to lie in her bathtub to rest her back.

I am indebted to many publications for information about Kahlo's life and paintings. The following were particularly useful: *The Diary of Frida Kahlo* (Bloomsbury, 1995), Hayden Herrera's *Frida: A Biography of Frida Kahlo* (Bloomsbury, 1989), Gannit Ankori's *Imaging her Selves: Frida Kahlo's Poetics of Identity and Fragmentation* (Greenwood Press, 2002), Martha Zamora's *The Letters of Frida Kahlo: Cartas Apasionadas* (Chronicle Books, 1995), and Denise and Magdalena Rosenzweig's *Self Portrait in a Velvet Dress: Frida's Wardrobe* (Chronicle Books, 2008) and their description of the unsealing of Frida Kahlo's bathroom/dressing-room in the Casa Azul in 2004.

Also by Pascale Petit

The Zoo Father

Shortlisted for the 2001 T.S. Eliot Prize, and a Poetry Book Society Recommendation, this unique collection centres on a daughter's fraught relationship with her dying father, a man whose legacy to her was violence and abandonment. Rich in the imagery of the Amazonian jungle (fire ants, shaman masks, hummingbirds, shrunken heads, jaguars) these poems at once ward off and redeem the father through myriad transformations. In contrast, 'The Vineyard' series is inspired by the author's mother and by "...the last piece of wild land, / left to me by accident, by dream" – a family vineyard in France.

These intense, vibrant and fiercely felt poems are sure to evoke strong responses in readers. Refusing oblique irony, quotidian props or any pretensions to urban hipness, Pascale Petit takes considerable risks. With fierce courage, she not only survives the brutal facts of her past, but transmutes them, through vivid imagination, into art.

> "A blazing new arrival" – Boyd Tonkin, the *Independent*, Books of the Year

> "This is a wonderful and red-raw collection that captures pain, love and loss." – *Independent*

> "Although rooted in real experiences, this is poetry that is deeply, wonderfully imaginative." – Poetry Book Society

The Huntress

In Pascale Petit's highly-charged third collection, a daughter is haunted by her mentally ill mother, and a painful childhood is re-imagined through a series of remarkable and passionate transformations. The feared mother is a rattlesnake, an Aztec goddess, a Tibetan singing bowl, a stalagmite, a praying mantis, a ghost orchid. These culminate in a long central poem where the daughter escapes her huntress as a cosmic stag. Underlying these poems is an intense mystical vision that lifts the dark material of the subject matter above the merely personal.

The Huntress was shortlisted for the 2005 T.S. Eliot Prize

"A brave and unsettling collection. These are psychological explorations of relationships and power struggles that take risks." – Robyn Bolam, *Poetry Review*

Pascale Petit
The Treekeeper's Tale

The Treekeeper's Tale

In contrast to the fierce confessional imagery of her first three books, *The Treekeeper's Tale* points towards another facet of the poet's gift, an intense feeling for the natural world, allied with a personal response to historical incidents and to other lands. The title section of this four-part collection adopts the giant coast redwood trees in California as a particular talisman. Lyrical, resonant, strange and imaginative, these poems echo in the mind and leave an indelible impression of the mysterious atmosphere of the redwood forests. The second section, 'Afterlives', takes us on journeys to the past, as in the burial of a Siberian priestess, and on trips to other places including China, Nepal and Kazakhstan. The colourful paintings of the German expressionist Franz Marc, such as the famous red and blue horses series, provide the key to the third section, 'War Horse', where dramatic imagery of the horses blends and contrasts with the tragic fate of Europe during World War One. The final part, 'The Chrysanthemum Lantern', features sensitive translations from Chinese originals.

"She operates a glittery, concise, deeply responsible magic realism, which explores the exotic, the wilderness and the faraway scrupulously for their own sake, but also as leaping metaphors for the relationships of home."

– Ruth Padel, *Independent on Sunday*

serenbooks.com

pascalepetit.co.uk

pascalepetit.blogspot.com